TATTOOS

ANNE SCHRAFF

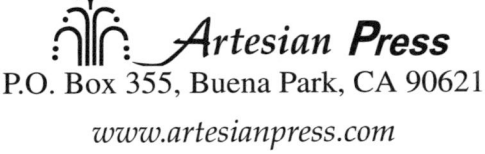

Artesian Press

P.O. Box 355, Buena Park, CA 90621

www.artesianpress.com

Nonfiction
eXtreme Customs Series

Body Modification	1-58659-211-4
Audio Cassette	1-58659-127-4
Audio CD	1-58659-361-7
Burials	1-58659-212-2
Audio Cassette	1-58659-128-2
Audio CD	1-58659-362-5
Fashion	1-58659-213-0
Audio Cassette	1-58659-129-0
Audio CD	1-58659-363-3
Food	1-58659-214-9
Audio Cassette	1-58659-130-4
Audio CD	1-58659-364-1
Tattoos	**1-58659-210-6**
Audio Cassette	**1-58659-126-6**
Audio CD	**1-58659-360-9**

Cover: www.wikipedia.org
Editor: John Bonaccorsi
Graphic Design: Tony Amaro
©2005 Artesian Press

www.artesianpress.com

 Artesian **Press**

ISBN 1-58659-210-6

Contents

Word List

Ainu (I-noo) Native people of the Japanese islands.

antiseptic (an-tih-SEP-tik) A substance that stops the growth of germs.

Dampier (DAMP-yer) A sailor and former pirate of the seventeenth century.

dermabrasion (der-muh-BRAY-zhun) The surgical removal of scars or tattoos that involves scraping the skin.

dermis (DER-mis) The layer of skin under the epidermis.

epidermis (ep-ih-DER-mis) The outer layer of skin.

hepatitis (hep-uh-TIE-tis) A serious disease that affects the body's liver.

Hildebrant (HIL-duh-brant) A German who tattoed soldiers during the Civil War.

irezumi (ee-reh-ZOO-mee) A Japanese style of tattooing, covering the upper body, arms, and upper legs.

Maori (MAUW-ree) Native people of New Zealand.

Omai (O-mie) A tattooed Polynesian man whom Captain Cook brought to England.

Polynesia (pah-luh-NEE-zhuh) A large group of islands in the Pacific Ocean.

Prince Giolo (JO-loe) A Filipino who had been taken by slave traders to Polynesia.

ritual (RICH-oo-uhl) A social custom or ceremony that is repeated and that has a certain form and follows the same rules, such as a wedding, for example.

Tahiti (tuh-HEE-tee) An island in the South Pacific Ocean.

tatau (ta-TOW) A Samoan ritual that would welcome a boy to manhood.

yakuza (YAH-koo-zah) Japanese gangsters.

Chapter 1

To Make A Mark

The boy lived in Samoa, an island in the Pacific Ocean. Having just become a teenager, he would be welcomed to manhood with a ritual (RICH-oo-uhl). It was called the tatau (ta-TOW).

Before the start of the tatau, men from the village gathered around the boy. They had all been through the ritual themselves, when they were his age; they kept telling him everything would be okay.

The tatau was long and painful. In it, the boy would be tattooed above his waist, around his legs, and around his back and sides. To make the tattoos, an artist would use traditional tools of bone, shell, and wood. Black ink would be used, and the designs to be drawn into the boy's skin would include triangles. The triangles represented the Samoan "flying fox," which is really a bat.

While the tattoo master worked, the men put their hands on the boy, to keep him still. They talked and sang to give him courage.

The master used a piece of sharpened bone to make the outline of each design on the boy's skin. He then hammered the sharp edge of the bone or of a shell against the skin, breaking it and letting dye sink in.

For two weeks after the tatau, a brother or close friend of the boy stayed with him. He helped him to bathe and to watch the many open wounds for signs of infection. After the tattoos healed, a feast was held to celebrate one more young man's journey into the adult world. The tattooed boy was now expected to take on many responsibilities, like those of the other men in the village. He would have jobs and help his family.

When you read that story of the Samoan youngster, you probably notice two things. First is that the word *tatau* looks and sounds like our word *tattoo*. In fact, our word comes from that word. Second is that the story is unlike any story you would hear of a boy in the United States.

In America, there are tattoos; but they are not usually part of a ceremony, as they were for the Samoan boy. In Samoa, the tattoos were a sign the young man had become part of the adult world. For some young Americans, tattoos are a sign of rebellion, a sign that they are no part of the world of adult expectations.

Although the meaning of tattoos varies with place—and with time—tattoos are nearly always to be found. There was a period, as we shall see, when tattooing disappeared from the Western world, which means from Europe and America. Eventually, it returned—and became more popular than ever.

Just what is a tattoo? A tattoo is a type of lasting mark made on the body; it may be a word, a design, or a symbol. We could say it is made "on" the skin, but that would not be quite right. It is made both "on" and "under" the skin.

Our skin has two layers. The outer one,

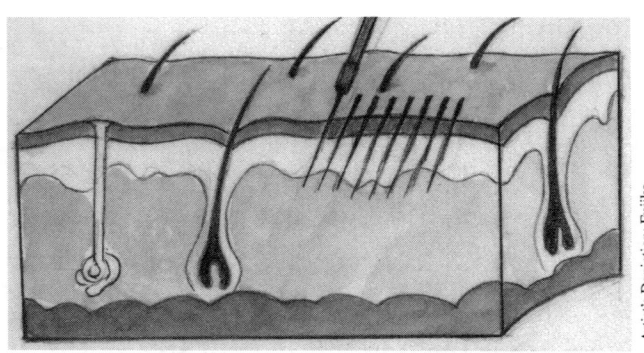

A tattoo needle punctures the skin's outer layer, to leave ink in the layer below.

which we can see and touch, is called the epidermis (ep-ih-DER-mis). It is our body's "wrapper"—thin and waterproof. Below that is a thicker, flexible layer called the dermis (DER-mis), which contains blood vessels and most of the nerves that give us our sense of touch. When a tattoo is applied, openings are made in the outer layer; and ink or some other colored matter is inserted through them. This pigment is captured down below, amid the cells of the dermis. Once it is there, it can be removed only by very-special means.

Although dermis and epidermis are modern, scientific names, the knowledge

10

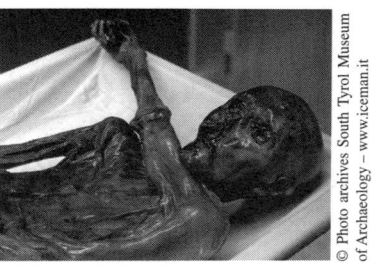

The Iceman was frozen in a glacier for 5,000 years.

that underlies tattoos arrived a long while before modern times. Pictures that seem to be of tattooed people in old cave paintings suggest that tattooing took place thousands of years before any history was written. Once people began to write down their history and began to become civilized, living in cities, tattoos were definitely a part of human life.

The earliest-known actual body marks that appear to be tattoos were found on the so-called Iceman, who was uncovered in 1991. The Iceman lived in the Bronze Age, an early period of civilization. For about 5,000 years, he had been frozen in a glacier in the high mountains between Austria and Italy, which are countries in Europe.

Several marks were seen on the Iceman's body. A band of small stripes was on his

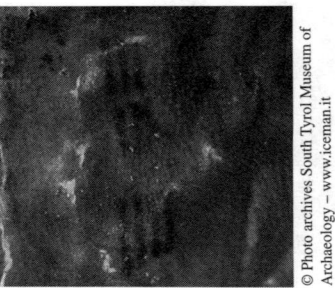

Parallel lines tattooed on the Iceman.

lower back, a cross was on his left knee, and more stripes were on his right ankle. All the designs were blue.

Some people think the Iceman's tattoos were decorations or had medical purposes; others think they were a sign of the man's importance in his tribe. The marks appear to have been made with charcoal. The tattoo artist might have believed he would ease the pain of an injury to the back or leg or prevent crippling in those parts of the man's body.

Around the time the Iceman was frozen into the ice, the civilization of ancient Egypt —one of the oldest on Earth—was rising. Tattooing was popular in Egypt. In the days when the pyramids were being built, Egyptians used needles to prick designs into their bodies. Clay dolls used by children as toys had tattoo marks that were the same as those of mummies with which they were buried.

A famous tattooed Egyptian priestess lived about 4,000 years ago, and her mummy was well preserved. Parallel lines were tattooed on her arms and thighs, and her stomach had designs that were like wide circles. Little statues buried with her were decorated in the same way.

The Egyptians had many ideas about tattoos. One notion was that tattoos were a link to the supernatural; they were created to honor the gods, or as a sacrifice to them. Many Egyptians believed tattoos gave magical or medical protection. A tattoo was better than a necklace or magic charm; it could not be lost the way a piece of jewelry could.

Chapter 2

Ancient Meanings

The custom of tattooing spread, probably from Egypt, to places near it, including Greece. When the Greeks rose in power, after the great days of Egypt, their civilization spread to many places; their spies communicated with each other through tattoos. A spy could read the tattoos on a newcomer and be able to tell he was a friend.

Once, a Greek who was being held prisoner by a Persian king sent his own son-in-law a message to start a rebellion against that king. He tattooed the message on a slave's head, which had been shaved. As soon as the slave's hair had grown back to hide the message, the "message" was sent on its way.

When the great days of Greece ended, a new power arose nearby—Rome. In Rome, tattooing was not for joyful purposes. Slaves and criminals were tattooed to make it more difficult for them to escape—and easier for others to catch them. Gladiators, who were forced to be in shows in which they fought against each other or against wild beasts to the death, were tattooed to show who owned them.

As you may know, those places—Egypt, Greece, and Rome—are all at the western end of the Old World. While tattooing was going on there, it was also going on at the other end, the part we Westerners call "the Far East." By about 4,000 years ago, tattooing had reached China, where civilization in the Far East began. There, tattoos were used the way they were in Rome—to identify and punish criminals.

Tattooing was not just for the peoples who lived in cities. To the north of civilization, from West to East, lived peoples who did not have cities at all. Civilized people called them barbarians. Although they lived in small settlements or roamed as nomads and

Artist's rendering of the tattoos on the barbarian mummy found in 1948

had songs and unwritten poems instead of books, they and the civilized peoples did have one thing in common: tattoos.

Near the western end of the barbarian area lived an ancient people in what is now southern Russia. The remains of one of their mummified chiefs was tattooed with wild animals. Farther to the east, in central Asia, a powerful, horse-riding people had tattoos. When the mummy of one of their chiefs was uncovered in 1948, it was found to have many connecting tattoo designs, mostly of strange beasts. Tattoos were later found on other

Ainu women, who lived in Japan, were tattooed with designs like big smiles. This woman's arms and hands are also tattooed.

Artist's Depiction: Fujiko

mummies from the same culture

All the way to the east were an unusual group of people who lived on islands that are now part of Japan but who were not ancestors of the people now called the Japanese.

This group is the Ainu (I-noo), who used tattoos to show off their social class and importance; a tattoo would basically tell strangers who a person was. Married women wore tattoos that told any man who might be looking for a wife that they were already taken. Girls who were growing up went through a tattoo ritual just as boys did. Modern descendants of these people show that the lips of the women were tattooed to look something like big smiles.

Eventually, ancestors of the modern Japanese moved into Japan. For many years, while they, too, were not yet civilized, they tattooed much of their bodies. Divers who went into the sea to get fish or shells wore tattoos they thought would scare off animals that might want to bother them.

When these ancient Japanese adopted Chinese civilization, they began to use tattoos as the Chinese used them: against criminals only. Someone who had committed a first crime had a line tattooed across his forehead. If he were to commit a second crime, an arch was added, and if a third, yet another line. Three lines across the forehead were the symbol for dog; they labeled the person an outcast who could not work or be accepted in normal society.

Chapter 3

Fading Away

Around A.D. 500, long after civilization began, life at the western end of the Old World took a big turn, a turn that affected everything—including tattoos.

As the power of the Roman government died away, barbarian tribes drifted—and sometimes stormed—into an empire that could no longer protect its borders. While this happened, Christianity, a religion that began in one corner of the empire, spread throughout what had been the Roman world. It replaced, in a way, the Roman way of life.

The Christian holy book, the Bible, has statements such as this: "You shall not... tattoo any marks upon you." Because of the belief that the body is a divine gift, which should not be marked in any way, tattooing in the Western world went out of favor. In fact, in the late 700s, the Pope, who was the leader of many Christians, forbade it. Tattooing in the Christian part of Europe disappeared.

When Christopher Columbus sailed from Spain in 1492, he was trying to prove that by heading west from Europe, he could travel around the world to reach the spice-rich lands of the East. Bumping into America instead, he began an Age of Exploration in which many other Europeans sailed out into the oceans of the world. Before long, those explorers were meeting new peoples, some of whom had something Europeans had not seen for hundreds of years: tattoos.

Explorers of Columbus's "New World" found tattoos among many of its peoples, who are now known as Native Americans. Christian missionaries, who came along with the explorers or soon after them, discouraged the Native Americans from tattooing. Eventually, tattoos all but disappeared among those peoples, the way they had disappeared in Europe centuries earlier.

This was not the end of tattoos; there

was yet another area in which they were widespread and from which they would exert a large influence. That was the Pacific Ocean.

The Pacific is Earth's largest body of water, and on many of the thousands of islands that lie in or around it live a variety of peoples. Several of those peoples, as the Europeans quickly discovered, had tattoos. The meeting of Europeans with those islanders was a large part of the unusual return of tattooing to the West.

The area of the Pacific whose tattoos had the biggest impact on Europeans was what we now call Polynesia (pah-luh-NEE-zhuh), which means "many islands." It is, indeed, hundreds of islands that spread across a triangle-shaped area that covers millions of square miles of ocean. Some of its islands have names you have probably heard: Samoa, which we have already mentioned; Tahiti (tuh-HEE-tee); Easter Island—even Hawaii, which is now part of the United States. Each of these places had its own tattoo traditions.

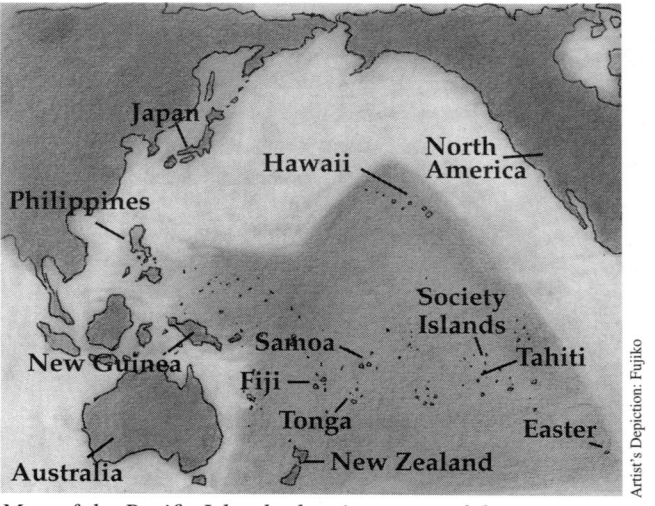

Map of the Pacific Islands showing many of the Polynesian settlements

In Samoa, sharks' teeth were sometimes used as tattoo needles. Some women had the tattoos put on their cheeks and the tattoo artist often struck the mallet too hard, pushing the shark teeth right through the skin of the cheek. That caused a deep scar.

To the Hawaiians, tattooing was a sacred practice, carried out while prayers were chanted. A tattoo was thought to offer supernatural protection. Because the right arm, which was used in hunting and in the

The faces of Maori chiefs are covered with carved tattoos.

hurling of spears during wars, was thought to need special protection, it was decorated with rows of tattooed dots. Tattooing the ankles offered protection against sharks.

In one corner of Polynesia is New Zealand. There, a people called the Maori (MAUW-ree) had a special kind of tattoo that both marked and carved the skin. This painful custom was sacred to them. Wealthy men could have their whole faces covered.

Chapter 4

Rediscovery

As you have probably noticed, tattoos are associated with sailors; even the cartoon character Popeye the Sailor had a tattoo—an anchor, on his forearm.

That should not surprise you. Sailors, who travel the world and see new things in faraway places, are often the first people to try foreign things. They bring back to their homes what they have seen in the wider world, as European sailors did in the case of tattoos.

In 1691, a sailor and former pirate named William Dampier (DAMP-yer) sailed from England to Polynesia. There he found Prince Giolo (JO-loe), a man who had been taken from the Philippines by slave traders. Giolo's body was almost entirely covered with tattoos, which Dampier thought would attract great crowds of curious people in

Prince Giolo drew crowds in London.

England. Dubbing Giolo "the painted prince," Dampier brought him to London, where he hoped to make a lot of money by presenting him to the public.

Giolo did draw great crowds, but not

Captain Cook

Engraving 1784 by J.K. Sherwin, after a painting by Nathaniel Dance.

for long. While he was exposing Europeans to something new and strange, they were exposing him to something with which he, in turn, was unfamiliar: smallpox. The disease had been in Europe for many centuries. Europeans did not realize they were carrying the virus that causes it to people who had never suffered from it, and whose bodies were not at all prepared for it. Giolo became one of many people who died of smallpox as they came into contact with Europeans.

In the late 1700s, about a hundred years after Giolo's journey to England, Captain

James Cook, a British explorer, made three voyages to Polynesia. Probably no explorer did more to help the world understand the geography of the Pacific, and probably no man's adventures are a larger part of the West's rediscovery of tattoos.

Everywhere Cook and his men went in Polynesia, they observed the art of tattooing. In North Island, which is part of New Zealand, they saw the unique Maori tattoo carving. They also saw that in Maori wars, tattooed heads of dead enemies were trophies. Heads of untattooed warriors were worthless and were kicked around the battlefield. Tattooed heads, which were preserved, were put on sticks and respected.

In January 1770, during Captain Cook's first voyage, Sir Joseph Banks, a botanist who was traveling with Cook, bought a tattooed head. Banks was a careful shopper, who chose the head from four he examined. When he took it back to England, he found that many people were interested in buying one like it. Europeans were soon offering the Maori large sums of money for more heads.

At first, the Maori had not wanted to sell that head to Banks; but when they saw the money they were being offered for more tattooed heads, some of them changed their minds. Before long, they were starting wars just so they could get heads to sell to Europeans. They sometimes traded heads for guns—to use during these wars.

One time, a European told a Maori chief he did not like the quality of the dried heads that were for sale. The chief told the man to look around at the living members of the village and pick out a tattooed head he liked. He promised the trader that, upon the trader's return, the head would be ready for sale—on a stick.

By 1831, the trade in human heads was so lively it was leading to widespread murder. It was soon declared illegal, and tattooed heads immediately lost their value.

Chapter 5

Cultural Exchange

After his first journey, Captain Cook had become very popular in London, partly as a result of the amazing stories he and his men told of the tattooing they had seen. They explained that the islanders used their bodies the way an artist uses a canvas—for beautiful artwork. They spoke of the black dye the Polynesians put under their skin to make the pictures, and they described the fruit of a nut that was the source of the dye. They spoke of Maoris whose legs were tattooed with so many black spirals that they appeared to be wearing pants even when they were naked. They described tattoo artists who used a flat bone or shell with up to twenty sharp points to puncture skin.

On his second voyage, Cook brought back living proof of the tattooed people. This was a man named Omai (O-mie), who

Omai appears before King George III and his wife, Queen Charlotte.

remembered some Englishmen from their visit to Tahiti, during Cook's first voyage.

In England, Omai was a happy man, who enjoyed teaching his English friends some Polynesian words. When he was not displaying his tattoos, he was dressed in the latest English fashions. The people of London thought he looked fine in English tweed suits.

Omai was brought to the palace and introduced to King George III and his wife. He learned to bow as the English do, and he even went to the opera and theater. He was seen at all the important dinners and parties. The famous artist Joshua Reynolds painted him dressed in an elegant turban and robes. He became a symbol of the pure-hearted native peoples of "the South Seas."

After about two years, Omai was getting homesick; he wanted to go back to Tahiti—or actually, to a neighboring island, where he had been born. In 1776, Cook set out on his third and last voyage, with Omai aboard.

When the voyagers arrived at Omai's home, Captain Cook tried to get Omai well-settled. He bought him land from the chief and planned out a garden for him. He ordered the ship's carpenters to build Omai a house made of planks. It was furnished with an English bed, tin pots and kettles, and a hand organ, which Omai played for the natives. Omai was given pistols, a musket, and some gunpowder, plus a horse, a mare, a saddle, and a bridle, which he knew how to handle well.

Little did Omai and Captain Cook know that their time was almost at an end. Omai was dead in two and a half years, and Captain Cook in half that. During that same voyage, after Omai had been dropped off, Cook discovered Hawaii. When a fight broke out between his men and the people there, he was killed.

Chapter 6

Back on Track

The death of Captain Cook was a shock to the people of England. As the British gained control of parts of Polynesia in the years that followed Cook's death, they discouraged tattooing. They knew tattoos were something that the Polynesians were proud of and that might encourage them to defy British rule.

This was a strange turn of events. After hundreds of years, tattooing in Polynesia was coming almost to a complete end, while in Europe, as a result of the contact with Polynesia, it was becoming popular again. In the islands, some of Cook's men had gotten tattoos and learned how to apply them. Back in England, they opened tattoo shops. Many rich people in England got tattoos. Many men got small tattoos so they could feel they were part of the ocean adventures they were hearing about.

Throughout the 1800s, tattoos gained popularity in Europe and America. Some years before the American Civil War, a German named Hildebrandt (HIL-duh-brant) moved to the United States and opened a tattoo shop. When the war was later underway, he moved between the lines, tattooing soldiers on both sides.

By 1882, English Queen Victoria's teenage grandson George, who eventually became King George V, had a tattoo. It was a dragon on his arm. Around the same time, Czar Nicholas II of Russia was tattooed, and in later years, King Frederick IX of Denmark was tattooed as well.

The tattoo craze had spread throughout England. Many men got tattooed and then joined traveling circuses to make money displaying themselves. Almost every sideshow in the country had an exhibit of tattooed people. In every traveling circus, in both England and parts of the United States, there was a tattooed lady. In later years,

Betty Broadbent

one of the most famous was Betty Broadbent, who was exhibited up to the early 1960s. Working with the Ringling Brothers and Barnum and Bailey and many other shows, she looked as though she were wearing a tattoo bodysuit. Betty's arms, legs, and part of her chest were covered with tattoos. In 1981, she became the first person to be honored by the Tattoo Hall of Fame.

Some years earlier, a man named Horace Ridler had been tattooed all over his body, including his face, with wide, zebralike lines. He had his teeth filed to sharp points and his nose pierced so he could wear an ivory tusk in it. Completing the change by having

35

Horace Ridler

his ears pierced and stretched, he called himself "the Great Omi." He was very popular for a long time. "Underneath it all," he would say, "I'm just an ordinary man."

Tattoos were still popular with sailors themselves, who wore them for many reasons. In choosing their tattoos, sailors liked symbols of the sea. A turtle tattoo meant a man had crossed the ocean. An anchor—such as the one worn by Popeye—was a sign he had sailed the Atlantic. A rooster tattoo on one foot and a pig tattoo on the other were supposed to save a sailor from drowning. That is because in real life, those animals don't swim. People believed that these tattoos would help get a drowning sailor onto dry land.

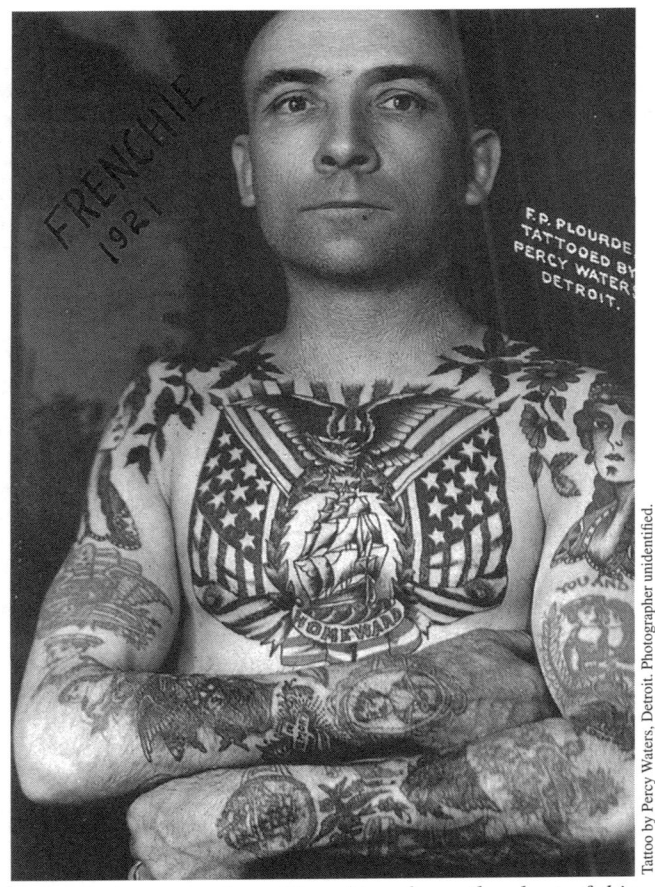

A patriotic tattoo of a sailing ship adorns the chest of this sailing man.

Tattoos of swallows were supposed to increase a man's skill in navigation. The number of swallows showed how far he had traveled on the high seas. One swallow meant he had gone at least 5,000 miles, and another swallow was added for each 5,000 miles after that. Sometimes a blue-green bird was used. Once a man had crossed the International Date Line, he was entitled to a tattoo of a dragon.

Tattoos were also used to identify a dead body in the years before DNA tests were possible. If a man's loved ones remembered the kinds of tattoos he wore, they could tell who he was in case his face had been destroyed.

Chapter 7

Rise of the Machine

Amazingly, tattoos were still being done the way they always had been: with simple tools. That was about to change.

In the late 1800s, a tattooist named Samuel O'Reilly bought one of Thomas Edison's inventions, the electric stencil pen. It was a needle whose point extended from the tip of a metal tube in which the needle was vibrated up and down by a small electric motor. Its purpose was to punch holes in paper, to make stencils of embroidery patterns and other things.

O'Reilly had bought the pen to make stencils of his tattoo patterns, so they could easily be transferred to the skin of customers. He realized he could use it not only to make stencils but also tattoos themselves. In 1891, having made changes that enabled the pen to hold ink that would coat the vibrating

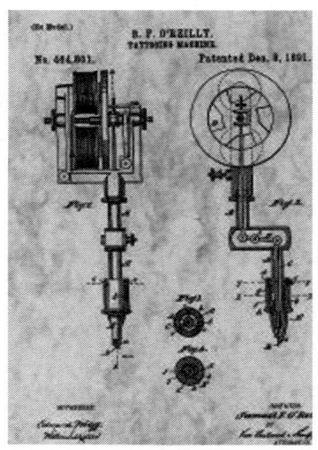

Patent drawing of Samuel O'Reilly's tattoo machine.

needle, he patented a device of his own: the earliest electric tattoo machine.

With O'Reilly's invention, tattooing no longer took a long time or caused much pain; so tattooing finally caught on with the general population. Unsurprisingly, this made tattoos less popular with upper-class people because tattoos began to seem "common." In the early 1900s, most "tattoo parlors" opened in the run-down sections of cities. They were found on streets with bars and other low-class places. Actually, most of the customers were still sailors, who, in that time, were expected to have tattoos. The best customers were young sailors, for whom tattoos were what they were for the Samoan boy: a sign of manhood.

40

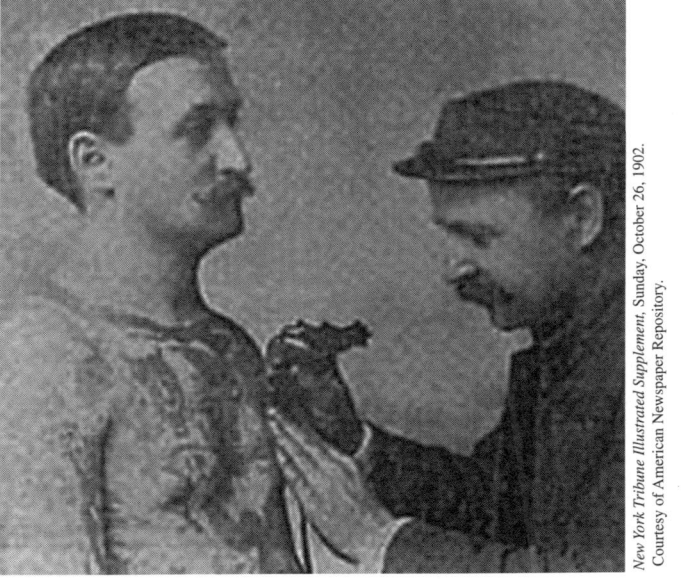

New York City tattooist of 1902

For the United States of the late 1800s and early 1900s, the center for tattooing was New York's Chatham Square. This was a seaport entertainment center with many tattoo parlors, including O'Reilly's. Charlie Wagner, Sam O'Reilly's helper, took over O'Reilly's tattoo parlor in 1908, and tattooing became more popular than ever.

Wagner teamed up with a man named Lew Alberts, who had been a wallpaper designer. Moving away from the patriotic designs that were popular in those days, Alberts created new tattoos, with images such as hearts, daggers, snakes, and flowers. He established what became the main American style for about fifty years. Alberts also started the practice of creating what tattooists call "flash." Flash are tattoo drawings that can be sold to tattooists who know how to apply tattoos but who might not be able to create designs of their own. Flash hangs on the walls of many tattoo shops.

Chapter 8

Losing Respect

Tattooing continued to grow. Tattooists offered cosmetic tattoos, which were done just to make someone more attractive. They created cheeks that always looked rosy, perfectly shaped eyebrows, and bright-red, beautifully shaped lips.

During World War II, in the 1940s, soldiers joined sailors in getting tattoos. Each branch of the military had its favorite symbols. Marines often chose bulldogs, or mottoes such as "Death before dishonor" and "Semper Fi," which means "Always Faithful." Imagine the power of such tattoos. Just as a Samoan boy had to live up to his tattoos and behave in a manly way, a Marine with such words on his arm would always be reminded of his duty.

Army men liked pictures of soldiers holding rifles. They also chose pictures of the Tasmanian Devil, an animal and a popular cartoon character. Sailors in the United States Navy adopted tattoos of girls, bluebirds, and Neptune, the ancient god of the sea.

In all branches of the service, military men often chose tattoos that were symbols of their own experiences. Sometimes, they would tattoo their rank and the names of places where they had served. Popular with the men of all branches was Lady Luck, a girl who looked like a hula dancer.

Wartime President Franklin Delano Roosevelt, who was known as FDR, had a tattoo of his family crest. John Fitzgerald Kennedy, a U.S. Navy man who later became president, had Irish ancestors, so he had a shamrock, a symbol of Ireland. Great Britain's wartime leader Winston Churchill had once been in charge of the British Navy; he had a tattoo of an anchor.

Tattooing was still a long way from being entirely respectable. In some dirty shops, a needle would be used over and over, on different people; so the practice got a reputation for spreading disease. At the beginning of the 1960s, there was evidence that, in New York, tattooing had caused cases of hepatitis (hep-uh-TIE-tis), a viral infection of the liver. In 1961, the city outlawed tattooing. Although some tattooing continued there illegally, the city's tattoo shops closed down.

Tattoos were also associated—as to some extent they still are—with criminals or other people outside "polite society." Persons in prison have their own tradition of tattoos. This is true in places besides the United States. During the years that Russia was a Communist country, called the Soviet Union, persons in prisons had tattoos that indicated the crimes they had committed. The tattoos became signs of honor. If a man wore a tattoo that indicated he had murdered someone, it had better be true. If not, one of the other prisoners might kill him for wearing a false tattoo. When the Soviet government collapsed, and the country became Russia

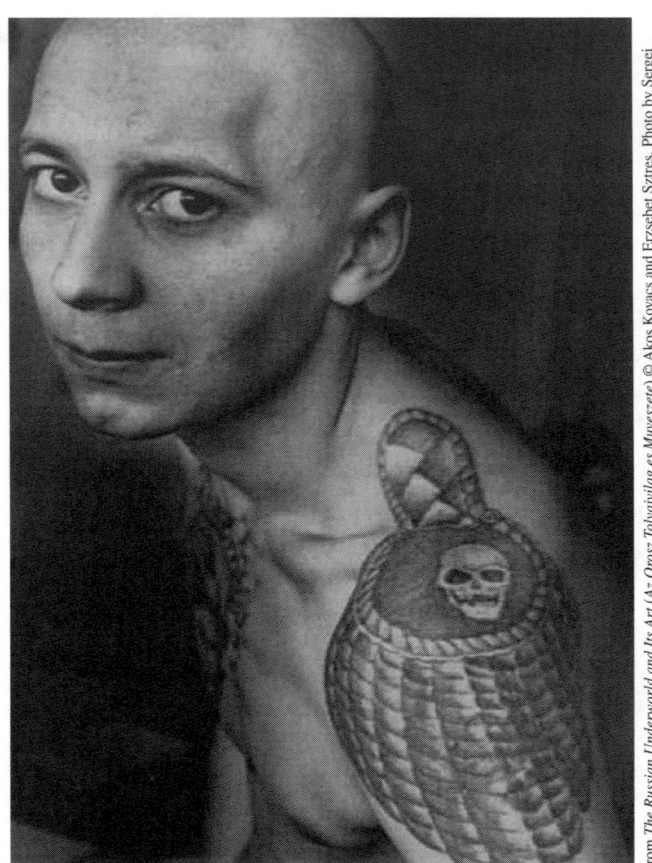

A skull tattooed on the shoulder of a Russian prisoner is usually the mark of a murderer.

again, criminals gained a lot of power. As a result, such prison tattoos became popular with some younger Russians.

Similarly, in Japan, tattoos are associated

46

Irezumi, which, in Japan, is favored by gangsters, is now being worn by regular persons in other countries.

with gangsters called yakuza (YAH-koo-zah). The yakuza like irezumi (ee-reh-ZOO-mee), elaborate tattooing that covers the upper body, the arms, and the upper legs. This style of tattooing became popular in Japan around the same time that Westerners were rediscovering tattoos; but when the Japanese government outlawed it in the middle of the 1800s, only gangsters continued to wear it. It is lawful now, but the connection with gangsters remains.

Tattoos in the United States are also associated with motorcycle groups. The members of each group proudly get a fancy symbol tattooed on their arms. Gang members use tattoos, too. A favorite symbol is a teardrop, which might mean time spent in prison or the loss of a friend.

Chapter 9

Respect Renewed

In the 1950s, Steve Allen, who was then the well-known host of television's *Tonight Show*, was tattooed on that program, which was broadcast live. The tattoo was four tiny dots, which were a symbol for "father." Tattooing then began to become popular with ordinary people.

By the 1970s, tattooing was very popular in the United States and in many other countries. Images that had once been widely used—the word Jesus, eagles, lions, tigers, panthers, and hearts pledging love to sweethearts or Mom—were replaced by a great variety of symbols and pictures. Some people honored friends by having their names or symbols associated with them tattooed on their own bodies.

Tattooing moved from the somewhat "underground" parlors—whose conditions were unhealthy—into everyday life. One of the groundbreaking artists was Lyle Tuttle, whose shop was in San Francisco. When he tattooed rock singer Janis Joplin, other celebrities followed her example.

Health risks associated with tattooing were not dealt with right away. The skin is the body's defense against infection, and any practice that involves breaking it is serious, requiring medical understanding.

In June 1992, APT, the Alliance of Professional Tattooists, was founded to protect the public's health and to preserve the professional standing of tattooists. Under APT rules, tattoo shops must meet all medical standards of cleanliness. Before being used, needles must be sterilized to make sure they are without germs. All needles must be disposable and must be thrown out after every use.

A person who wants to get a tattoo can check with the APT to see whether the tattooist he or she wants to use is a member. The person getting the tattoo must take the responsibility to be alert to the conditions of the tattoo shop and the equipment being used there. A sloppy tattooist who uses dirty needles and equipment that is not sterilized can spread serious, even deadly, infections. As you might guess, the smart tattooist takes steps to protect not only customers but also himself or herself. During tattooing, the customer does bleed a bit and the blood can carry dangerous germs.

Tattooing is now part of the modern world, and even though its basics have not changed, it is done in ways that involve modern knowledge and technology.

At the beginning of the process, the skin that is to be tattooed is shaved and is then cleaned with an antiseptic (an-tih-SEP-tik) solution. The antiseptic stops the growth of germs that are living unseen on the epidermis; that way, the tattooing will not drive them down below, where they can cause infection.

In the next step, a stencil is pressed onto the skin. It leaves a purple outline of the

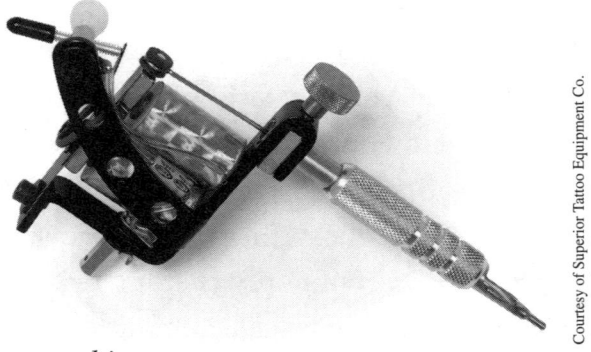

Tattoo machine

planned tattoo. If the person to be tattooed likes the outline, the tattooist will proceed.

After putting on medical gloves, the tattooist holds the tattoo machine by the tube that surrounds the needle. When he or she dips the tube's long, narrow tip into a tiny bowl of ink, some ink rises into the tube, the way water rises into a straw that has been placed in a glass of water. Natural forces hold it there.

Positioning the machine at the customer's skin, the tattooist turns it on with a foot switch. As the needle rapidly vibrates, up and down, ink runs down along it. If the speed of the machine is set too high, the needle will bounce off the skin. If everything is set right, the needle punctures the skin as the tattooist moves the machine steadily along to create the tattoo.

Small dots of blood come to the skin's surface, as when skin is pricked with a pin. The customer feels a burning sensation. If excess ink runs onto the outer skin, it blocks the work from the view of the tattooist, who pauses to wipe it away with a cloth. From time to time, the tattooist must also switch the machine off for another dip of ink.

A simple tattoo can be applied in as little as 30 minutes. More-detailed tattoos can take several hours. As soon as the tattoo is finished, the skin is cleaned and a light ointment is put on it. A loose bandage is placed over the fresh tattoo, and the tattooed person receives very specific instructions about caring for the wound. Any sign of swelling or fever might signal an infection and should alert the person to go to a doctor right away.

Chapter 10

Sign of the Times

In the 1990s, tattoos surged in popularity and respect. Maybe nothing symbolized this better than New York City's 1997 decision to make tattoo parlors legal again. Tattooing became a thriving industry and art form.

In the United States alone, there are now tens of thousands of professional tattooists. A talented tattooist can make a good income. Art museums around the world hold shows about tattoos. Every year, thousands of people attend the many tattoo gatherings that are held in different countries. The artistic power of the best tattoos impresses many people.

In design, there are several types of tattoos. There is, for instance, the flat style, which is usually black with no shading. Known also as the "new tribal" style, it offers simple symbols. Geometric figures such as

The best tattoos have artistic power.

circles, squares, and triangles are often seen, as are organic shapes. Although it can be very striking, the flat style can also look just like a lump of color without detail.

Another style is the American traditional, whose designs are somewhat like those of the middle of the twentieth century. Using thick black outlines and solid blocks of color, it is sometimes called "neo-traditional," which means "new traditional." Popular themes are daggers, hearts, girls, snakes, and flowers. This style is visually attractive, especially from a distance.

A third style is fine-line tattooing, which,

as its name suggests, uses narrower, fine lines and greater detail. More-serious artists like this style because of the delicate designs. It is richer in color and content than other styles and is more realistic than they are, but from a distance it may look too busy and confusing.

For a long time, the wearing of tattoos in the Western world was mostly limited to men, but now many women are being tattooed as well. In fact, women get 40 percent of the tattoos done in the United States. Flowers and butterflies are popular choices.

Cosmetic tattooing—done just for beauty reasons—is more popular now than ever before. Eyeliners are tattooed onto women's eyelids, so that ordinary eyeliner does not have to be put on every day. Eyebrows are plucked and then replaced by tattooed eyebrows of a desired shape. The need to apply lip liner each day is done away with by the tattooing of a permanent line. Some women even have beauty marks tattooed onto their faces.

Obviously, a woman who gets such "permanent makeup" will be in a difficult position if she decides she would like a different appearance. Indeed, any person who is no longer pleased to be wearing a particular tattoo—especially a tattoo that is not easily covered by clothing—is in difficulty. Getting rid of a tattoo is neither easy nor cheap.

At the moment, there are four basic ways to remove tattoos. The acid peel burns off layers of skin with chemicals, but it is very painful. Dermabrasion (der-muh-BRAY-zhun), which is also painful, involves scraping off the tattooed skin to reach the unmarked skin below. Surgery is a third method, in which the tattooed skin is cut out. This is drastic and can lead to infection or scarring.

The most common method involves the use of lasers, which produce powerful pulses of special light. Passing through the layers of skin that bear the tattoo, the rapid pulses break up the dye. Removal of the tattoo

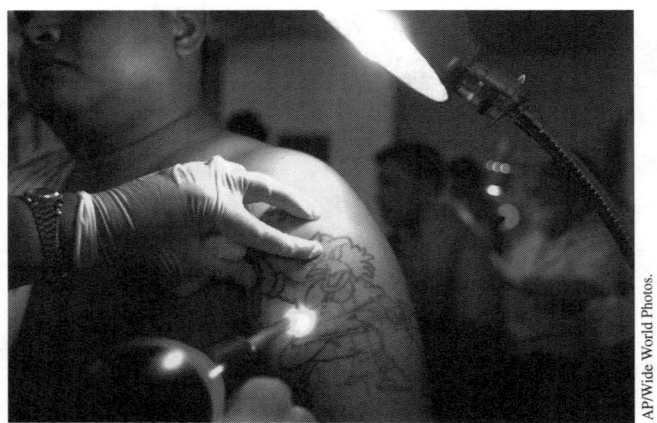

Tattoo removal by laser

requires two to eight treatments, spread four to six weeks apart. The intervals allow the dye time to be flushed out of the body. This costly method has been compared with being spattered with hot oil, and it does not guarantee the tattoo's complete removal.

In the modern age, as we have seen, people get tattoos for as many different reasons as there are designs. Some people are simply excited by the decoration of their bodies with tattoo art. Some are tattooed to show they belong to a certain group or gang, others to show they stand apart.

Most tattooed people are ordinary men

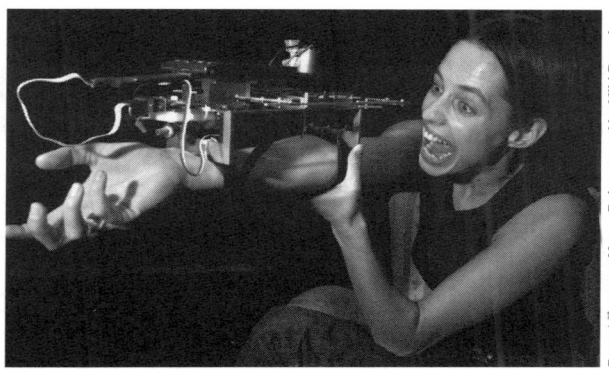

Central European News. Robot created by Niki Passath. Model: Sanna Tobias.

Ancient art, modern tool: tattooing robot

and women, who may have simple, personal reasons for getting tattoos. Many are like the young woman who, after a streak of bad luck, had an angel tattooed on her shoulder to watch over her. Some are like the young man whose tiny dot tattoo on the palm of his hand was special to him because the ink used to apply it was made from the ashes of his grandfather.

Of course, there are also many people who would never consider getting a tattoo and who do not even like to see tattoos on others. Tattoos are simply not for them. Even so, tattoos seem unlikely to vanish. They're under our skin.

Bibliography

"Bishop Museum, Honolulu, Hawaii—A History of Tattoo." http://www.coldsteel.co.uk/articles/bishop-museum.html

Blumberg, Rhoda. The Remarkable Voyage of Captain Cook. New York: Bradbury Press, 1991.

Burkett, Kyle. "The Rise and Fall of a Western Stereotype." Urban Folklore, 2001.

Channel, Carrie. "The Tatau: A Bridge to Manhood." Faces, May 1, 2002.

Eldridge, C. W. "Tattoo History from A to Z." Tattoo Archive. http://tattooarchive.com/tattoo_history.htm

Finan, Eileen. "Is Art Just Skin Deep?" Time International, April 29, 2002.

Foreign Prisoner Support Service. "Russian Prison Tattoos." http://www.phaseloop.com/foreignprisoners/exp-russian_tats.html

Gilbert, Steve. "Tattoos." Seaport: New York's History Magazine, Summer, 1995.

Kaeppler, Adrienne L. "Tattooed Beauty: A Pacific Case Study." Anthro-notes (Winter 2001).

Krakow, Amy. The Total Tattoo Book. New York: Warner Books, 1994.

Lloyd, J. D., ed. Body Piercing and Tattoos. San Diego, Calif.: Greenhaven Press, 2003.

Miller, Jean-Chris. The Body Art Book: A Complete, Illustrated Guide to Tattoos, Piercings, and Other Body Modifications. New York: Berkeley Books, 1997.

Schildkrout, Enid. "Body Art as a Visual Language." Anthro-notes (Winter 2001).

Additional Information Provided by:

C.W. Eldridge, Tattoo Archive, Berkeley, California

Dora Karolyi, Hungarian Book Foundation, Budapest, Hungary

Gil and Rae, Tattoo Odyssey, Philadelphia, Pennsylvania

M. Jankowski, Lisa Marie Jankowski, Panama City Florida Research, Reference, and Referral Services. circlearts@aol.com